Britney Spears
Stylin'!

Maggie Marron

WARNER BOOKS

A Time Warner Company

DEDICATION:
To Nellie and Kellie

Warner Books, Inc., 1271 Avenue of the Americas, New York, NY 10020
Visit our Web site at www.twbookmark.com
Ⓦ A Time Warner Company

Printed in the United States of America
First Printing: November 1999

10 9 8 7 6 5 4 3 2 1

ISBN: 0-446-67583-0
LC: 99-64588

Editors: Emily Zelner and Ann Kirby
Photography Editor: Valerie E. Kennedy
Book Designer: Jennifer O'Connor
Cover Designer: Carolyn Lechter
Production Manager: Camille Lee

Contents

Introduction

Take one part small-town girl, one part impeccable style, and one part hit record, and what do you get? Britney Spears. Many believe that this sweet Southern belle from Kentwood, Louisiana, became an overnight star when her first album hit number one—but by that time, Britney was already a show business veteran.

Friends and fans agree that one of the best things about Britney is that despite her superstardom, she's still the same old girl. She loves hanging out with her friends at the mall when she goes home, talking on the phone, and playing board games. She may be the girl all the guys want to date, but she's down to earth enough that girls still love her like a best pal. If you met her on the street, you would probably think she was just your average, ordinary, everyday teenager. But Britney has a plan. As she told Donna Freydkin, a reporter for CNN Interactive, "I want to conquer the world."

That's no small feat, but it looks like she's on her way. At the ripe old age of seventeen, Britney has achieved what no other new female artist in music history has—she's the first female (and the youngest artist ever) to have a simultaneous number-one debut album and single.

Britney loves the limelight and the glamour. She loves the excitement of being on the road too, but when she's away, she misses her family and friends and her mom's cooking. But Britney has already learned that she can't sit home and be a normal teenager. "God gave me a talent to perform and I know I have it in me. I can't just coop it up," she says. Music lovers everywhere can thank God for that!

Britney Spears, the girl next door.

CHAPTER ONE
Small-Town Girl

We Are Family

Britney Jean Spears was born on December 2, 1981, to Jamie Spears, a construction contractor, and Lynne Spears, a second-grade teacher. Britney and her mom are very close. The young star told *Girl's Life*: "My mom is so sweet. She helped me become who I am, and she taught me to have strength. I have to talk to her every day." But Lynne Spears has never been a stage mother. "Her parents were not pushing her at all," says Jeff Fenster, a senior vice president at Jive Records, recalling one of his first impressions of the Spears family.

The middle child of three, Britney has great relationships with her older brother, Bryan, and her baby sister, Jamie Lynn. Bryan, in typical big-brother fashion, admitted to *Rolling Stone* that "it was very annoying" when Britney did most of her performing in front of the family's television set in the early part of her career. But despite having to watch many of his favorite television shows through little Britney's whirls and jumps and turns, Bryan loves his little sister the same way most big brothers do. He protects her—even though she bugs him. "He is a good brother," Britney told *Girl's Life*. "He is sometimes the father type, always looking out for me. Sometimes he drives me crazy." And despite the eleven-year difference in their ages, Britney has a great relationship with Jamie Lynn, who is now showing signs of becoming a performer herself. She often joins her big sister in family room productions—and sometimes she even does her own solo numbers when Britney's not around.

One of the best things about Britney is her adorable smile. No one who meets her can resist its charm.

Softly angled bangs. Wearing her hair in a high ponytail with wispy bangs framing her face draws attention to Britney's warm eyes and gorgeous features.

Subtle makeup. When Britney's in casual mode, you'll find her wearing nothing but soft earth tones on her flawless complexion.

Pretty in pink. Britney loves wearing clothes that complement her hair and skin tones, and pink is a real winner for this light brown-haired beauty!

The wardrobe staple. Britney loves to lounge around in her favorite pair of jeans, which are soft, faded, and perfectly broken-in.

PERSONAL STYLE

We found Britney in her casual duds, which are a far cry from the outfits she wears to perform. Britney loves being comfortable. She wears clothes that "give" and are easy to dance around in. Jennifer Aniston and Jennifer Love Hewitt are two of her top fashion icons, and her favorite store is the GAP—just like most girls her age! Follow the tips above to achieve Britney's casual look.

Britney loves to layer snug tank tops with loose-fitting crocheted sweaters. ABOVE, *she arrives backstage in style, wearing a chic cardigan and khakis.* OPPOSITE, *Britney wears a similar ensemble as she strikes a dreamy pose during a photo shoot promoting her smash album,* ...Baby, One More Time.

Full name: Britney Jean Spears
Date of birth: December 2, 1981
Star sign: Sagittarius
Hometown: Kentwood, Louisiana
Parents' names: Jamie and Lynne Spears
Brother: Bryan
Sister: Jamie Lynn
Pets: A rottweiler named Cane
Nicknames: Bit-Bit, Brit

Hair: Light brown
Eyes: Brown
Height: 5 feet 4 inches (162.5cm)
Weight: 105 lbs (39.2kg)
Hobbies: shopping, movies, riding her go-cart, swimming, going to the beach
Favorite singers: Whitney Houston, Mariah Carey, Madonna
Dream date: Ben Affleck

FORMER MOUSKETEER BUDDIES —THEN AND NOW

In her two-season stint as a Mouseketeer on the Disney Channel's remake of *The Mickey Mouse Club*, Britney rubbed elbows with more than one soon-to-be star. Among the most famous to date are Keri Russell, the star of television's *Felicity*, and, of course, JC Chasez and Justin Timberlake of 'N Sync.

Keri donned her mouse ears from 1991 to 1993, having one season of overlap with Britney. When *MMC* was canceled, Keri moved to Los Angeles to pursue her career. Before she won the role of a lifetime in *Felicity*, Keri guest-starred on several sitcoms, including *Boy Meets World* and *Married...With Children*.

'N Sync's Justin Timberlake and JC Chasez also worked with Britney on *MMC*, and because they're all so close in age, they hung out together a lot. 'N Sync has become an international sensation seemingly overnight, but the guys still attribute much of their success to their time on the show, as they admitted to their fans in a 1998 AOL online chat session. JC called *MMC* "...the experience of a lifetime. We got to do all spectrums of the business, not just singing and dancing, but acting, too. It's something that will be with us for the rest of our lives. It was a great experience." Justin added that he "...definitely think[s] it helped with our music because we got to sing a lot on the show."

The Mickey Mouse Club *has been the springboard for many young rising stars ever since it debuted in the 1950s. Britney joined the cast in 1991, a year before Keri Russell (front, center) left the show.*

Britney grew up in Kentwood, a very small Louisiana town (population: 2,600) about an hour north of New Orleans. Although Britney has nothing but fond feelings for her hometown, she feels more at home in the big city. "Growing up in a small town, you tend to have more values—you can take your time," she explained in an interview with *Teen Celebrity*. "But I've spent a lot of time in New York City, and I wouldn't change that for the world." The best part is that when she goes home, people treat her like she's still the same old Brit—and she is. She wouldn't have it any other way.

Starlight, Starbright

Britney always knew she was going to be a star. At the age of two, when most toddlers are just starting to speak in full sentences, she was singing into hairbrushes in the bathroom mirror. "She was always singing—she would never hush," Lynne Spears told *Rolling Stone*. Britney's mother realized her potential early on and enrolled her in dance class at age four. At five, Britney was the diva of her kindergarten class, belting out "What Child Is This" at the graduation ceremony.

Britney is as comfortable in front of a camera as she is on stage—which is a good thing, considering the countless photo shoots she has to sit through!

"I was always pushing my parents when I was young. By the time I said it was time to go to New York, they were well aware of how much I wanted to

Eat your heart out, Sporty Spice! Athletic Britney has played her share of sports—she's earned her right to wear a jersey!

Small-Town Girl

𝓑RITNEY 𝓠UIZ #1

1 Who does Britney thank first in her acknowledgments for her first album?

    a. her mother, Lynne

    b. her lawyer, Larry Rudolph

    c. God

    d. Jive VP Jeff Fenster

2 How many copies did Britney's debut album sell its first week out?

    a. 35,000

    b. 125,000

    c. 500,000

    d. 800,000

3 What's Britney's fave song to perform?

    a. "…Baby, One More Time"

    b. "Sometimes"

    c. "Soda Pop"

    d. "Crazy"

4 Who is Britney's favorite actress?

    a. Demi Moore

    b. Meg Ryan

    c. Drew Barrymore

    d. Jennifer Love Hewitt

5 Finish the line: "Oh baby, baby, how was I supposed to know…"

answers: 1: c; 2: b; 3: c; 4: d; 5: "…That something wasn't right here."

The former mousketeer really loaded up on souvenirs for her family and friends when she participated in Disney's Easter parade in May 1999.

Small-Town Girl

succeed," Britney has confessed. But for all her drive and ambition, Britney was able to enjoy a fairly normal childhood. A dedicated student, she won a perfect attendance award in second grade. She took dance classes (jazz), gymnastics, and voice lessons. She had lots of friends and even played on her junior high school basketball team. Britney comes from a very religious family and is highly devoted to her Baptist faith. She sang in her church choir as a young girl, and one of her first demos was a religious song.

Throughout elementary school, Britney performed in talent competitions and was the princess of many a Kentwood parade. She won her first competition in August 1990 at the Bellmont in Baton Rouge, Louisiana. Girls from four states—Texas, Alabama, Mississippi, and Louisiana—competed. Eight-year-old Britney danced, sang, and did gymnastics, and was the overall winner for all age groups. In 1992,

The hotties of 'N Sync, from left: Joey Fatone, Justin Timberlake, Chris Kirkpatrick, JC Chasez, and Lance Bass. Justin and JC became pals with Brit while they were performing on The Mickey Mouse Club, *and later when they toured together.*

Britney won the Miss Talent USA competition singing "There, I've Said It Again." This title earned her a tiara, trophy, banner, flowers, a check for $1,000—and a chance to appear on *Star Search*, the famous weekly televised talent show hosted by Ed McMahon, twice that same year! She also did her share of national television commercials.

Like Britney, former Mousketeer JC has toured the world, singing and dancing on stages from Kalamazoo to Crete, where this photo was taken.

Britney got an audition for the Disney Channel's revival of *The Mickey Mouse Club* in 1990, but at eight years old, she was much too young to be a Mouseketeer, even though the judges responded to her talent and charm. Luckily, one of the producers recognized Britney's star quality and introduced her to a New York City agent. Lynne Spears temporarily moved to New York with her two daughters so that Britney could pursue some acting opportunities and get more experience and exposure. Britney started spending summers in New York, attending the Off-Broadway Dance Center and the Professional Performing Arts School. In 1991, she landed a role off-Broadway in *Ruthless*, a comedy based on the 1956 thriller *The Bad Seed*. "At ten I was playing this really bad child who seems real sweet but she's evil, too," she remembers. "It was so much fun."

Britney auditioned once again for *The Mickey Mouse Club* in 1992 and was finally selected. During her stint as a Mouseketeer, Britney got to work with future stars Keri Russell (of the television drama *Felicity*), Justin Timberlake, and JC Chasez (both members of the rock band 'N Sync). Of Justin and JC, Britney told *Girl's Life* that despite all that's "...happened to them...they are basically the same." But she quickly added, "Actually, JC has matured a lot. He's quieter now than he was. On *MMC*, he was totally rambunctious. Justin is the same." Britney admits to being

Britney shared the Mickey Mouse stage for one year with Keri Russell, who now plays the lead on TV's Felicity. *Of Russell's on-screen persona, Britney says, "Isn't she breathtaking? So cute!"*

great friends with all the guys from 'N Sync, but says she's closest to Justin and JC because of the time they spent together on *MMC*.

When *Girl's Life* asked Britney how she remembered Keri Russell, she responded "She's so sweet. She's a beautiful person." No doubt that's also how Keri, or anyone else who knows Britney, would describe her.

Just two years after Britney earned her mouse ears, *MMC* got canceled and she returned home. She enrolled in a nearby private school, which was quite a change from her show business life. "Remember that opening scene in *Clueless* with all the cliques? That's what it was like," she confessed to Steven Daly of *Rolling Stone*, though in his article he does confirm that she got along with everyone, "cheerleaders and burnouts alike." No surprise from everyone's favorite girl!

Britney's next chance to break into the limelight came when she auditioned for an all-girl group in New York City. Meanwhile, Lynne Spears had sent a demo tape of her daughter's singing to entertainment lawyer Larry Rudolph, who got Britney an audition with Jive Records. These events would be key in Britney's journey to superstardom.

"When people see things on TV that they can't do, that should make them want to go out there and make something of them-selves. That's how I looked at it."
(**Rolling Stone**, *April 15, 1999*)

Brit's taste in jewelry is elegant simplicity. Notice that all the adornment this natural beauty will allow is tiny stud earrings, a delicate pendant, and a bracelet.

CHAPTER TWO
A Star Is Born

Eye of the Tiger

When word came that Britney had an audition lined up to join an all-girl band, which she adamantly denies was modeled after the Spice Girls, she was overjoyed. You can take the girl out of the spotlight, but you can't take the spotlight out of the girl. As much as Britney loved spending time with her parents, siblings, and Kentwood friends, she felt like a bird with her wings clipped. "It was fun for a while," says Britney, "but I started getting itchy to get out again and see the world." Britney needed to perform, and Kentwood was just not going to give her that opportunity. So she packed herself up again and headed for New York.

Her audition for the band was very successful—she got in. But she only did it for a day. Why? Britney told Stephen Lenz of *Teen Celebrity* that "…they couldn't get their dance numbers together. But then I got signed at Jive Records, and since the group didn't even have a name, I thought it made more sense to take advantage of the recording opportunity."

Smart move. No one knows whatever happened to that group, but today, everyone knows the name Britney Spears!

Britney's lawyer, Larry Rudolph, sent a demo of Britney singing to Jive Vice President Jeff Fenster. "She sang over an instrumental that wasn't in her key—but I heard something special," Fenster told *Billboard* magazine. "Her vocal ability and commercial appeal caught me right away." Fenster hooked Britney up with writer-producer Eric Foster and later reported that "they came up with some incredible stuff."

Britney in full-force performance mode. A truly athletic dancer, she's not afraid to break a sweat when she performs—that's how she stays in such great shape!

The up-do. When Britney performs, she likes to keep her hair out of her face. A high ponytail looks stunning on her, even as wisps fall out from jumping around on stage.

A Britney trademark. The tied-up, sporty shirt is both stylish and practical. Not only does it let her show off her great abs, but the knotted shirt keeps her cool and comfortable while she jumps around beneath the hot stage lights.

Hip Huggers. Brit wears her drawstring khakis slung low on her hips. A small transmitter belted around her waist allows her to "wear" her microphone, instead of having to carry it around while she dances and sings.

DANCE STYLE

Britney's been dancing since her mother started her in lessons when she was just a toddler. Today, she still gets her best workout with her dancing shoes on! Follow the tips above to master Britney's workout style.

IT'S IN THE STARS

How well does Britney fit her star sign? It looks like more than just a little bit. See how Britney measures up!

SAG	BRIT
Sagittarians strive for self-expression and they need many diverse outlets	Britney is a talented singer, dancer, and actress
Sagittarians relish speeding down the road of life on the quest for adventure and knowledge	Britney is already a superstar at seventeen—and wants to learn all she can about the entertainment business
Sagittarians are gregarious, generous, and cheerful	Britney is gregarious, generous, and cheerful
Sagittarians like to work independently and mix work with travel whenever possible	Britney chose to be a soloist even though she was accepted into an all-girl group— and of course, she loves to travel!
Sagittarians have dominion over areas of their bodies designed for locomotion	Britney is a talented dancer and loves exercise
Sagittarians can't stand to be bored	Britney is truly happy performing

Sagittarius:

Dates: November 22 to December 21
Element: Fire
Planet: Jupiter
Birthstones: Sapphire, turquoise
Colors: Shades of blue and violet

What do Sagittarians look for in a partner? They need someone who's pioneering, courageous, exciting, enthusiastic, and who can keep up with them both intellectually and energetically.

Are you compatible with Britney? You could be if you are an

Aquarius (January 21 to February 19), Aries (March 21 to April 20), Leo (July 21 to August 23), or Libra (September 24 to October 23)

Fenster was very impressed by the sweet, young, Southern belle, whose talent was accompanied by a determination to succeed. "For any artist, the motivation—the 'eye of the tiger'—is extremely important," Fenster explained to *Rolling Stone*. "And Britney had that. This is clearly a self-motivating person from a very young age."

Baby One More Time

Britney had a great time making her debut album, especially because she was working with Eric Foster (a man who had worked wonders with the likes of Whitney Houston and Hi-Five, among other Britney favorites) and Max Martin, producer of the Backstreet Boys and Ace of Base. "It came together rather quickly, unusually so for a pop album," Fenster told *Billboard*. "It was a case of good chemistry among a group of very talented people. The writers and producers immediately saw what we at the label did: Britney is a star."

The next step after recording the album was deciding which single would be released first—and then filming a video for it. "…Baby One More Time" was chosen. Then it was just a matter of nailing down the right video concept.

According to *Rolling Stone*, the original idea was far off from what Britney had envisioned. "They had this really bizarre video idea, this animated Power Ranger-y thing," Spears told Steven Daly. "I said, 'This is not right. If you want me to reach four-year-olds, then OK, but if you want me to reach my age group…' So I had this idea where we're in school and bored out of our minds, and we have Catholic [school] uniforms on. And I said, 'Why don't we have knee-highs and tie the shirts up to give it a little attitude?'—so it wouldn't be boring and cheesy." (By the way, that's really Britney putting her gymnast training to good use, doing her own backflips in the video!)

Yellow tie, tied-up shirt, bright orange plaid pants. The school-girl look that Britney perfected for her "...Baby, One More Time" video was pioneered during her 1998 mall tour.

SMALL-TOWN GIRLS MAKE THE BRIGHTEST STARS:
Britney and Her Pop-Music Idols

Now, we already know that at seventeen, the pretty and talented Britney Spears topped the charts with her debut album. But

Mariah Carey

it's also true that at least three of her pop-star inspirations came from similarly humble beginnings and became full-fledged divas at relatively young ages! What does Britney have in common with some of her favorite pop stars? More than you might guess.

Aside from talent and charm, Britney has business sense, savvy, and ambition that just won't quit—traits she shares with Mariah Carey, Whitney Houston, and Madonna.

Like Britney, Mariah Carey had always known that she wanted to sing and dance and be a big star. She grew up in Huntington, New York, a small town on the eastern part of Long Island. Mariah was born to an Irish-American opera singer and African-Venezuelan engineer on March 27, 1970. As a singer, Mariah's mom always encouraged her daughter's talent—the same way that Lynne Spears encouraged Britney—and by age fifteen, Mariah was singing the New York City club circuit. She got her big break when she landed a back-up gig with Brenda K. Starr.

Mariah released her debut pop album, *Vision of Love*, in 1990, at the ripe old age of twenty. That album took home two Grammys and boasted four number-one singles! For her second album, Mariah wrote all the songs herself, something Britney dreams of doing one day. And that was only the

A Star Is Born

Whitney Houston

New Jersey. From there, she went on to sing backup for such famed singers as Chaka Khan and Lou Rawls. Meanwhile, she regularly modeled for *Seventeen* magazine during her teenage years. But singing remained her true love. By the time she was twenty-two, Whitney had been signed by Clive Davis of Arista Records and released her self-titled first album, *Whitney Houston*, in 1985.

Audiences went wild for the bright new singer, and her second album, *Whitney* (1987), was the first album by a female artist to ever

beginning: Mariah has stayed in the spotlight and maintained her reputation as a prolific and talented songstress.

Like Mariah, Whitney Houston also had a musical background and a family that loved to sing almost as much as she did. In fact, Whitney's mother is famous gospel singer Cissy Houston, and her aunt is pop diva Dionne Warwick. Like Britney, Whitney first sang in public in her church choir, in her hometown of Newark,

Madonna

debut at number one. (Britney holds the record for being the first female artist whose *first* album debuted at number one.) Throughout the 90s, Whitney continued to release hit albums, including *I'm Your Baby Tonight* (1990) and the soundtrack for the motion picture *The Bodyguard* (1992), in which she starred with Kevin Costner. This album sold an unprecedented 16 million copies, and the single "I Will Always Love You" spent fourteen weeks at the coveted number-one position on the charts. We predict that Britney will surely enjoy similar success with her future projects.

Perhaps one of Britney's biggest idols is the Material Girl herself, Madonna. And what better model could there be for a young singer who's just as talented a businesswoman as she is a performer? Madonna left home at nineteen and struggled as a performer in New York City until she got her first real break with the 1982 single "Everybody." She went on to become one of the wealthiest, most famous, and most powerful women in the

Britney, princess of pop

music industry. Several number-one singles and albums as well as key roles in feature films would follow in the next fifteen-plus years of her superstardom. Not bad for a gal from the suburbs of Detroit, Michigan!

Will Britney achieve the permanence and superstardom of her pop-diva idols? Only time will tell, but it looks like there's no doubt in anyone's mind: Britney's here to stay!

"Drink lots of water, eat well and get
lots of sleep….After all that, my skin's
usually in top form."
(Teen Celebrity, *Summer 1999***)**

How has Britney responded to any flack she's received from the video's sexy concept? "All I did was tie up my shirt!…I'm wearing a sports bra under it. Sure, I'm wearing thigh-highs, but kids wear those—it's the style. Have you seen MTV? All those girls in thongs?"

Needless to say, the video, like the song, is a phenomenal success. Britney's ability to get her way and influence the winning concept for the video shows that she is a budding diva and a shrewd businesswoman who's not afraid to speak up to make her work better.

It's only part of the reason that critics and fans agree that Britney's star won't burn out, causing her to fall into oblivion. The other part is that she's fiercely determined to never let it happen to her.

When the recording was complete and the video filmed, only half the work was done. Now it was time for promotion. Jive pulled out all the stops to celebrate its potentially brightest new star. Even though the album wouldn't be released until the beginning of 1999, promotions began in the summer of 1998. Jive wanted to get audiences hungry for Britney—and it worked.

For a sophisticated yet business-like look, Britney sports a pinstripe suit with a dainty camisole peeking out.

Jive started by mailing out several thousand postcards printed with a Britney Website, email address, and toll-free 800 number that offered samples of Britney's songs and interview soundbites. "We put that number on postcards and circulated them to the fan clubs of several major pop artists," confessed Jive's director of marketing, Kim Kaiman, to *Billboard* magazine. "The response was tremendous, without even having a single in the market. Kids were intrigued by Britney."

Kaiman continued, "We knew that we had this great package—a gifted singer who could dance like a dream. We knew people would go for her once they saw her." What followed was a marathon tour of twenty-six malls in twenty-eight days, sponsored by *YM*, *Teen*, *Seventeen*, and *Teen People*.

Britney toured America's malls with two dancers and goody bags full of promotional materials and teaser cassettes to further gear up record buyers. "It went over like gangbusters, drawing hundreds of kids in every market," reported Kaiman. "You can't dictate to kids. They're independent buyers—and they really went for Britney big-time."

Like Fenster—or anyone else who comes into contact with Britney—Kaiman was impressed by Britney's incredible drive. "I have never seen an artist so focused on what she needed to do," she told *Rolling Stone*.

Britney had a great time meeting fans on the mall tour. "No one knew who I was, but I could see they really enjoyed the music," she told *People* magazine. "And I got a lot of shopping done." But probably the most important thing to come out of the mall tour was the way it helped prepare her for the next leg of her promotional campaign: touring with megastars 'N Sync.

A Star Is Born

ℬRITNEY 𝒬UIZ #2

1 What famous duo first performed "The Beat Goes On?"

   a Sonny and Cher

   b Steve and Eydie

   c Donny and Marie

   d Salt-n-Pepa

2 What's Britney's favorite ice cream flavor?

   a chocolate chip cookie dough

   b rocky road

   c strawberries and cream

   d mint chocolate chip

3 Favorite color?

   a sea green

   b baby blue

   c bright orange

   d hot pink

4 Who is Britney's favorite author?

   a Stephen King

   b Judy Blume

   c Sandra Brown

   d Danielle Steele

5 Finish the line: "I'm looking at a picture in my hand…"

answers: 1: a; 2: a; 3: b; 4: d; 5: "…Trying my best to understand"

"*I want to be an artist that everyone can relate to, someone who's young, happy, and fun.*" (Teen Girl Power, *March 1999*)

A then-unknown Britney performs during her 1998 mall tour.

CHAPTER THREE

Into the Spotlight

On the Road Again

As soon as Britney completed her mall tour in the summer of 1998, it was time to really get down to business. At this point, she was almost a household name among teens, but her album had not yet been released and "…Baby One More Time" had only just started to grace the airwaves. But Britney was making a name for herself with her killer dance moves, enchanting singing voice, undeniably sweet personality, and fierce determination.

In the late fall of 1998, Britney toured with 'N Sync to get her fans geared up for the release of her album. Although sometimes the media tries to link Britney romantically with any one of her 'N Sync pals—especially Justin Timberlake—she says they are just friends. "They're really cool guys. They're so completely normal. Their success hasn't changed them at all, which is really good," she told *Teen Beat* in a recent interview.

The tour started in early December and ran for more than two months; that was longer than Britney had ever been on the road without going home. Generally, Britney likes traveling, but it does have its drawbacks. "I don't do normal things due to the travel, and the biggest sacrifice is being away from my family," Britney told Donna Freydkin of CNN Interactive, "but I wouldn't change anything in my life."

Luckily, Britney has a great relationship with her friends, who aren't jealous of her success at all and treat her just like they always have, no matter where she is. "[My friends] are great," Britney told *Girl's Life*.

Sing it baby, one more time!

Up-and-down hair. With her hair pulled back just on the sides, Britney can perform with her hair looking long and glamorous, but it won't get in her way when she dances.

A less casual look. Britney wears more makeup when she performs, as the hot stage lights can make anyone look a bit pale. Here, dark gray and silver eye shadow bring out her eyes, while bold cocoa lipstick accentuates her perfect smile.

The cropped top. Here, Brit sports a black velvet athletic-cut pant suit. The cropped top— along with a faux navel piercing— show off that toned stomach.

PERFORMANCE STYLE

It was Britney's idea to get dolled up in a Catholic schoolgirl's uniform for her "…Baby, One More Time" video. And that schoolgirl look caused quite a stir among her critics and fans alike. But Brit makes no apologies, and continues to call her own shots when it comes to her wardrobe. It's very important to Britney that she wear just the right outfit when she's being filmed or performing. Jot down some of the tips above to model your own performance style after Britney's!

"Things I would wear [in New York], I would never wear at home. People would look at you and think you were crazy. Here, if you walk out with purple hair, it doesn't really matter."
(Teen People, April 1999)

Performing gives Brit lots of opportunities to try on different looks. Chic and retro, Britney looks like a young Cher when she performs her cover of "And the Beat Goes On."

"We keep in touch, call each other, and keep up with the gossip. When I come home, we go for rides to the beach, you know, do fun girl stuff."

Britney had a great time with her 'N Sync pals on the tour. But although she doesn't mind touring, it can really take a toll on her. "The first week it was really weird and you're just getting adjusted to being on the bus and not getting that much sleep," she told *Teen Beat*, "but I'm getting used to it. I love being on the road."

Britney also admitted to CNN Interactive, "Most of the time when I'm on the road it's crazy. I'm trying to do photo shoots and interviews. But I'm always trying to make some time for a little shopping."

'N Sync and Britney shared a tour bus, which made the traveling even more fun: "I like being on the bus. I have four dancers with me, two guys and two girls, and we just goof off and have so much fun, we act like total goobs… [But] sometimes you get in really, really late, or I can't sleep and we have to be at a radio station at, like, six in the morning and I've gone to bed at four and feel really exhausted the next day."

If Britney hit any of those radio stations or made any other appearances while in a cranky mood, no one ever noticed, as Jive's senior vice president of pop promotion, Jack Satter, can attest. "The truth is that she shook the hand of every possible pop programmer in this country," he told *Billboard* magazine. "She's a charming young woman and a hard worker. Factor in a great record—a very aggressive, reactive record—and you can't miss."

Undaunted charm aside, Britney had never before performed in front of audiences of the sizes that attended the 'N Sync shows. Sure, she was a seasoned stage performer and had already sung her heart out

Britney didn't have to feel nervous on the road during her first tour—after all, she was opening for her old buddies, the boys of 'N Sync.

Britney has denied in the past that she's dating 'N Sync hottie Justin Timberlake...

...but recent rumors suggest that the two are an item.
And what a couple they make!

All That Jive

The label that discovered Britney Spears has a great track record in finding other talented acts. Jive has made a commitment to supply the teenage world with hot music and even hotter stars.

One of the label's biggest acts, the Backstreet Boys, began as a trio—Nick Carter, Howie Dorough, and A.J. McClean—that performed an *a cappella* act in Orlando. When they hooked up with Kentucky cousins Kevin Richardson and Brian Littrell, they became the Backstreet Boys (named for an Orlando market) and began singing together throughout Florida.

The Boys were soon swept up by former New Kids on the Block managers Donna and Johnny Wright, and they signed with Jive in 1994. Jive started the guys out in Europe and Canada in 1996, and by early 1997, their debut album, *BSB*, was released in the United States, debuting at number twenty-nine. To date, the album has sold more than ten million copies worldwide. Their new album, *Millennium*, is breaking records around the globe! And if you keep Britney's album running past the end track, "And the Beat Goes On," you'll be able to sample a couple of tracks off the new Backstreet Boys album!

Another of Britney's fellow Jive acts is 'N Sync, who are also managed by Donna and Johnny Wright. Britney had loads of fun touring with her label-mates during her 1998 tour, and despite the experience of watching thousands of girls her age go crazy for the guys, she hopes to tour with them again soon! "I've been backstage as their opening act, and I've been out there or whatever, and girls out in the audience are lifting their shirts up, and I'm dying. I'm like, 'Oh my goodness, I'm not believing this. This is bad,'" reported *MTV News* online.

Britney's old friends Justin Timberlake and JC Chasez of *MMC* fame as well as Joey Fatone, Chris Kirkpatrick, and Lance Bass, have become the latest heartthrobs.

OPPOSITE: *Britney performs at New York radio station Z-100's Jingle Ball in December 1998.*

Like the Backstreet Boys, they were also launched in Europe (they were most popular in Germany and the Netherlands) before their self-titled first album hit the United States in 1998. 'N Sync's debut album held the number-two spot to Britney's number one in mid-January of 1999.

Jive Records continues to be a wellspring of hot young talent in the music industry. Jive will also be putting out Britney's next album.

Britney and members of 98° strike a pose for paparazzi at the Jingle Ball.

on national television, but this was much different. Thousands of crazed teenagers at a time—mostly girls—were overcome with anticipation waiting for their boys to perform. And Britney had to warm them up. "My first time up on stage was nerve-racking," Britney has admitted. "I was so scared that I was going to forget my dance steps or the words to the songs! After a while, though, it became much easier."

Overcoming stage fright doesn't mean that all her performances have been perfect. All stars have had their share of embarrassing moments, Britney included! During one of her shows, Britney was wearing a flight suit that her dancers were supposed to pull off, but it didn't come off, no matter how hard they pulled. Her

𝓑RITNEY 𝓠UIZ #3

1 What's Britney's favorite song?

- **a** "Like a Virgin" by Madonna
- **b** "Purple Rain" by Prince
- **c** "The Greatest Love of All" by Whitney Houston
- **d** "Control" by Janet Jackson

2 Favorite beverage?

- **a** Sprite
- **b** Peach Snapple
- **c** Orange Juice
- **d** Coke

3 What's Britney's favorite movie?

- **a** *There's Something About Mary*
- **b** *Gone With the Wind*
- **c** *Titanic*
- **d** *Ten Things I Hate About You*

4 Where does Britney really like to shop:

- **a** The GAP
- **b** Bloomingdales
- **c** Macy's
- **d** K-Mart

5 Finish the line: "But you put a dart through my dreams, through my heart…"

answers: 1:b; 2:a; 3:c; 4:a; 5:"…And I'm back where I started again. Never thought it would end."

Britney arrives backstage at the Z100 Jingle Ball in New York City. She always makes time for a few photographs!

second embarrassing moment left her even more red-faced. Britney was performing after B*witched, and someone in the audience had put a cupcake on the stage. Poor Britney never saw the sweet treat and slipped and fell on it. "It was so crazy," she blushed. "I was so embarrassed! Luckily, T.J., one of my dancers helped me up. That was one of the most embarrassing—but funniest—moments in my career!"

Despite these humbling moments, Britney told *Teen Girl Power*, "I love performing more than anything and having people hear my music. I know I've had to give some stuff up to do this, but I don't miss high school. When I was home two years ago, every weekend we'd go out and do the same thing. It's wonderful as long as you love what you're doing, but I'd rather be doing this."

Top of the Pops

Britney's last sold-out performance with 'N Sync was in Biloxi, Mississippi, on Sunday, January 17, 1999. She spent the afternoon signing autographs in a local Wal-Mart, and although she was pretty tired by then, she was full of energy and charm for the hundreds of local fans who came to get her signature.

About the tour, Britney said, "It's been an incredible, intense time. It hasn't always been easy opening for these guys, since there are all girls in the audience. But I ultimately am able to win them over. I have guy dancers, too, and believe me, that helps." And Britney did win the girls over, perhaps more than she realized.

By the middle of January, she was able to return home for a few weeks before heading out for an international tour. But there would be many surprises in store for her in the coming weeks. Britney's album had just been released and her single was getting lots of airplay, but she had yet to hear it on the radio. She told *Teen Beat*, "Everyone at home had been hearing it, but

we were so busy that we hadn't had a chance to hear it on the radio. So when I got home, we got in the car and it came on. It was so weird. I was like 'Oh, yay!' I started screaming like a big goob. It was neat. It was really neat."

But there were more surprises in store for her. Just one week after her album's release, it soared all the way to number one. The very same week, "…Baby One More Time" also grabbed the top spot on the singles charts. Britney had set a new record for young female performers—and she didn't even know it!

By simply adding a cowboy hat, a bouquet of flowers, and a teasing pout—Britney changes her entire look.

When Britney finally found out that she was the top of the pops, she was shocked. "Omigosh, I was overwhelmed. When they told me, I went, like, 'Whaaa?'" she reported to *Teen Beat*. "I'm like really thankful—really, really happy about everything," she told *Rolling Stone* online. "I never really expected it to go to number one with the single doing so well, I was just gonna be happy if it went on the charts."

PREVIOUS PAGES: *Touring the world does have its perks. Here, Britney and a buddy catch some rays on board a Sunseekers yacht on the Mediterranean during the Monaco Music Festival.*

Pop music's reigning queen, Miss Britney Jean Spears.

CHAPTER FOUR
Number One and Going Strong

Forever Starstruck

Even though Britney is riding high these days on her flourishing fame, she hasn't lost touch with her sweet, unassuming, unpretentious self. Despite mountains of fan mail, she's still starstruck when she spots celebrities.

When she's in Los Angeles, she can't even get a cup of coffee without bumping into one "because every time we go, we see somebody famous," Britney told Veronica Chambers for *Newsweek*. "I saw the guy from 'Tommy Boy' [David Spade].… He was just standing there and drinking coffee. It was really weird."

In New York, Britney bumped into a few more celebrities. "I was like, 'Oh my gosh! Tori Spelling!' She was walking down the street with that guy she is dating on the show. I was so freaked out. I also saw Prince [one of her favorite singers] and Scary Spice [her favorite Spice Girl]. I was totally starstruck," she confessed to *Girl's Life*.

Of course, it hasn't really all settled in yet that she, too, is just as famous, which is part of her irresistible charm and part of the reason why millions love her. But the reality is starting to sink in. "The first time I went home…the single had just taken off. I noticed all these people coming up to me in stores and stuff…," she told *Rolling Stone* online. "I was always on the road and I was never going out in public. And it was, 'Uh, oh. This is a little crazy.' But it was flattering, too.

Britney looked like a princess at the 1999 American Music Awards.

A crown of curls and jewels.
A new look for Britney, with her hair wavy and pulled back in a bejeweled headband to match her dress.

Perfect makeup. Brit's makeup is never overdone and always just right. Britney chose a palette of soft earthy tones for her makeup on this special night—shades of brown eye shadow and coral lipstick.

A stunning sheath. An ankle-length, perfectly form-fitting, white beaded gown—as always, Britney looks elegant and beautiful.

GLAMOUR STYLE

Britney is having a great time at the top of the charts, but her seemingly overnight fame hasn't really changed her one bit. She still loves hanging out in her casual clothes when she's at home or hanging out with her pals in the shopping mall, but she also loves dazzling fans by wearing glamorous clothes. She wore this gorgeous ensemble when she was a presenter at the 1999 American Music Awards. Is this the kind of look you'd like to have for your prom or special dance this year? If so, check out these tips for creating Britney's glamorous style.

The woman of a thousand gorgeous looks. Britney performs "And the Beat Goes On" with her dancers at the Monaco Music Awards.

I think after a while it'll probably be annoying." For now, it doesn't seem to bother her. She told *Girl's Life* that "the best is when you get free stuff, like ice cream. Silly things like that are the best."

But like any celebrity, Britney is afraid of becoming too famous. What scares her the most is "losing my identity and my privacy. How fun can it be going out with friends when your bodyguard is right there all the time? I've started to notice people staring at me. That's a little weird."

Time Out

Britney was stuck at home for a while because she hurt her knee during a rehearsal for a new video. She was happy to be spending time with her family, but she started getting a little antsy. She was supposed to be on a world tour, but instead she was home, watching television and taking some downtime waiting for her

Brit performed at the World Music Awards in Monte Carlo in a sequined pantsuit. Like her idol, Madonna, she likes to change her look to suit the number she is performing.

leg to heal. Britney still managed to be upbeat. She didn't mind being a normal teenager for a little while, and she enjoyed hanging with her old friends, playing board games, going to the movies, or just chatting on the phone.

THE WORD IS OUT

— Britney Spears is H-O-T! So What Are People Saying About Britney's Number One Album?

"It's got one of those 'I can't get it out of my head' hooks that just makes you want to get up and dance."
— Andrew Jaye, Program Director/Music Director
WEOW, Key West, Florida (from Billboard*)*

"Even after hundreds of spins, it's unshakable. It's a pure pop record that our listeners simply cannot get enough of."
— Clarke Ingram, Program Director
WPXY, Rochester, New York (from Billboard*)*

"Hanging ten on the sugary wave is 17-year-old ex-Disney princess Britney Spears, who sounds so soulful and Whitney-assured, it's downright scary."
— Tom Lanham
Entertainment Weekly online

"Oh bay-bay, bay-bay, Ms. Spears has herself a mega-smash
CD...Britney won't be starving for hits, that's for sure."
— Michael Slezak
Teen Celebrity

As much in love with her fans as they are with her, Britney signs autographs and stops to wave and smile before a taping of Late Show with David Letterman *in May 1999.*

"You want to be a good example for kids out there and not do something stupid." **(Rolling Stone,** *April 15, 1999)*

Britney was thrilled to become a model for Tommy Hilfiger—her favorite fashion designer! Here, she and Tommy show off his spring 1999 line. Doesn't that jeans-and-camisole ensemble seem perfect for her?

One of the real bummers about being laid up, however, was that she couldn't get out and actively promote her album. But that didn't seem to make a dent in record sales. "I'm so happy it's been up on the charts for so long," she told CNN Interactive. "I mean, so many albums don't stay up there and I hope that mine does, and it's great."

While Britney was recuperating at home, she did whatever she could to promote the album from her living room sofa: she gave interviews and happily spoke to the press. Britney's been getting her share of flack, though, from critics and fans who think the photos she took for *Rolling Stone* are too sexy—especially for someone so young. That doesn't seem to bother Britney—or her parents—one bit. As she told *MTV News* Online, "*Rolling Stone*, they tend to push the envelope a little bit, and that's cool because it's *Rolling Stone*… And I've seen other people on the cover and it's like, 'Whoa!' But it's okay. I wouldn't do this for any other magazine, but because it's *Rolling Stone* I think it's fine and tasteful."

Moving Forward

Britney is not going to stop until she gets to the top, and even then, she's going to strive to go further. "I'm working hard every day and I feel truly blessed," she reported to CNN

Recording an album may seem like all fun, but it's really a lot of hard work. Brit dresses casually when she's in the studio.

So many clothes, so little time! Britney found herself in Tommy Girl heaven—a wardrobe full of Hilfiger jeans and other clothes—during shoots for the Tommy Jeans '99 ads.

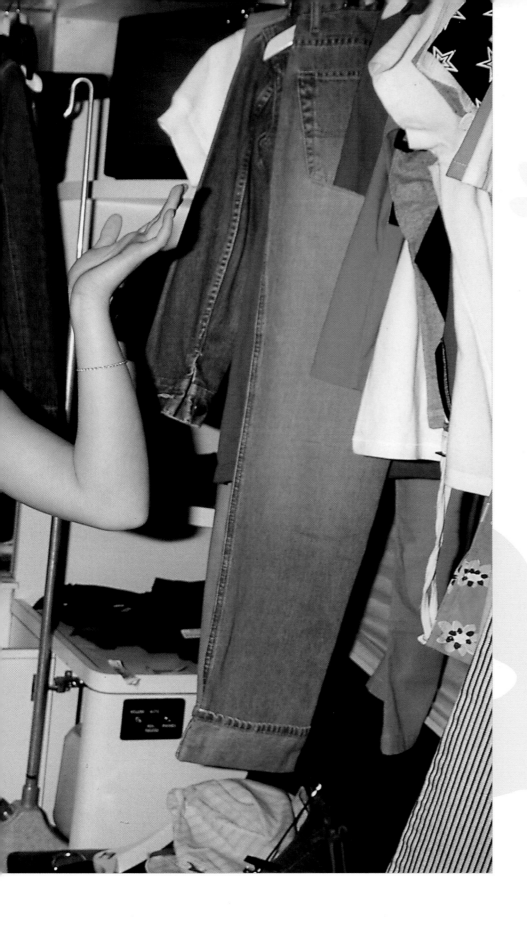

"I don't recall getting any prom invites this year," Britney told Teen Celebrity *in 1999. "I guess everyone knows I'm a little busy." Lucky for Britney, her career gives her lots of opportunities to go formal!*

Interactive. As Britney told *Billboard* in December of 1998, "I've been working toward this moment for a long time. I just want to keep on building and building."

Even while working toward this not-so-modest goal, Britney has found time to explore the limelight outside her usual medium. She ventured into the world of modeling when she signed with Tommy Hilfiger to represent his spring 1999 collection. And Britney returned to television when she filmed a number of episodes of *Dawson's Creek* for the fall 1999 season. And yes, she played herself. "I'd definitely want to play a sweet girl—as opposed to a mean character—because I wouldn't want to lose any of my fans," Britney told reporters when news broke about her stint on *Dawson's Creek*.

Looking a little wiped out from her first tour, Britney is never too tired to talk to an interviewer—or have her photo snapped.

Britney is also experimenting with writing her own music. Although she didn't write any of the songs on her first album, she has assured the

**Britney's advice for
pop-star wanna-bes:
*"...you have to love what you are
doing and you have to love to sing.
If so, then go for it."*
(Girl's Life, *February/March 1999*)**

public that that's changing. "I was so young when I began," she admits. "Subsequently, I was really scared to try some of my own stuff. Now that I have a bit of experience under my belt, I want to try something new. It's time to begin recording my own material." Don't forget to check the B sides of Britney's singles for some of her songs. "Sometimes" features the Britney Spears original "I'm So Curious."

Some interviewers have asked Britney if she thinks she might change the style of the music she performs for her next album, perhaps become more gritty like Alanis Morrisette or a more rock-and-roll type like Sheryl Crow. But Britney feels that pop music is what suits her best. "I want to stick to it, you know," she told *MTV News* Online. "Pop music is me, because I can dance to it...when I first got signed, we knew I was going to sing pop music...before Natalie Imbruglia came out, that's the kind of music I wanted to sing."

Britney enjoys a mid-tour cruise in the Mediterranean.

Number One and Going Strong

ℬRITNEY 𝒬UIZ #4

1 What's Britney's favorite sit-com?

   a *That 70s Show*

   b *Friends*

   c *Zoe, Duncan, Jack, and Jane*

   d *Just Shoot Me*

2 What is Britney's favorite book?

   a *The Bridges of Madison County*, by Robert James Waller

   b *The Shining*, by Stephen King

   c *Star*, by Danielle Steel

   d *Little Women*, by Louisa May Alcott

3 Who is Britney's favorite basketball player?

   a Patrick Ewing

   b Larry Byrd

   c Michael Jordan

   d Dennis Rodman

4 Who is Britney's favorite actor?

   a Brad Pitt

   b David Duchovny

   c George Clooney

   d Michael J. Fox

5 Finish the line: "Tell me I'm not in the blue …"

Answers: 1:b; 2:b; 3:c; 4:a; 5:"… That I'm not wasting my feelings on you."

"It's so awesome just to hear your song on the radio and see your video on MTV. This is unreal." **(People Weekly, February 15, 1999)**

Britney all dolled up for the Monaco Music Awards. This beautiful beaded ball gown looks great with her hair highlighted to a shiny honey-blonde.

As competitive as the business is, this young star knows that she will succeed. In a few years, no one's going to ask, "Whatever happened to that Britney what's-her-name?" because she'll still be putting out number-one hits. Britney has been compared to 1980s teen sensations Tiffany and Debbie Gibson, whose pop careers lasted little more than one or two albums each, but she thinks the comparison isn't really fair. "I think I'm more grounded, you know. I know what I want out of life and my morals are very strong. I have major beliefs about certain things and I think that has really helped me cope with stardom," she has said. And whether or not she's the next Tiffany, well, Britney has said, "We're totally different people, and our sound is totally different." Luckily, most critics and fans agree.

Britney receives tons of fan mail from guys and girls alike. The girls usually compliment her on her singing voice or her style, and sometimes warn her to "stay away from my boy, Justin," to which she playfully writes back, "No problem!" But the guys…well, the guys are something else altogether. Britney told *Teen Beat*, "They say things like 'marry me!' Marry me? I don't even know you!"

As for life outside her career, Britney has decided to put a lot on hold in order to focus on her music. Britney knows that eventually she will need to take a break to go to school. "I do want to go to college," she promises. "But right now I want to focus on my music. I agree that a person needs a college education to fall back on—besides, this business is crazy!"

For now, she's going to enjoy her superstardom. "You get so pumped and it's awesome and you get so much energy," she told CNN Interactive. "The best part of doing this is when the fans are touched by you and know the words to all your songs."

Actress, singer, dancer, songwriter, businesswoman, and all-around nice girl: for Britney Spears, the only way to go from here is up!

BIBLIOGRAPHY

Periodicals

Andrews, W.C. "Britney Spears Signs Autographs Before Concert." *Knight-Ridder/Tribune News Service.* (January 19, 1999).

"Britney Spears." *Teen Girl Power.* (March 1999):70.

Brown, Ethan. "Teen People Gives Newcomer Britney Spears the Cinderella Treatment and Turns Small-town Girl Into a Stunning Pop Princess." *Teen People.* (April 1999):126-127.

Chambers, Veronica, with Gill James. "Pop's (Sexy) Teen Angel." *Newsweek.* (March 1, 1999):64.

Daly, Steven. "Britney Spears: Inside the Mind (and Bedroom) of America's New Teen Queen." *Rolling Stone.* (April 15, 1999):60-65, 129-131.

Flick, Larry. "After Quiet Build, Jive's Teen Star Spears Breaks Out." *Billboard.* (December 12, 1998):1.

Helligar, Jeremy, with Michael Haederle. "A Major Minor: Singer Britney Spears, 17, Flexes Her Muscles in the Booming Teen Music Market." *People Weekly.* (February 15, 1999):71.

"Hit Sensations Presents Britney Spears: Britney Hits the Big Time." Hit Sensations TV Series Presents vol. 1 no. 22. *Fanzine International*, New York.

Lenz, Stephen. "Britney Spears." *Teen Celebrity.* (March 1999):46.

"Britney Spears: Who Better Than This Teen Phenomenon to Dish Prom Tips?" *Teen Celebrity.* (Summer 1999):43-47.

Mayfield, Geoff, Keith Caulfield, and Steve Graybow. "Teen Queens." *Billboard.* (February 13, 1999):116.

Novak, Ralph. Review of "...Baby, One More Time." *People Weekly.* (February 1, 1999)

Sanders, Heather. "From the Bottom of Her Heart." *Girl's Life.* (March 1999):26-28.

Thiggpen, David, E. "A Sweet Sensation: Killer Abs and an Army of Producers Put Britney Spears on Top. Will Fans Love Her Tomorrow?" *Time.* (March 1, 1999):71.

"We're All Ears for Britney Spears." *Teen Beat.* (June 1999):37

World Wide Web

absolutecelebrities.com. Keri Russell Biography, c. 1998.

America Online. Transcript of online chat with 'N Sync. (April 24, 1998).

Boehlert, Eric. "Baby, One More Teen: 16-Year-Old Britney Spears Goes from Shopping Malls to No. 1." *Rolling Stone* online. (January 20, 1999).

Britney Spears bio, peeps.com/bmg.com, c. 1999 BMG Online.

Freydkin, Donna. "Pop Princess Britney Spears Sets Out to Conquer Music." Special to CNN Interactive. (March 24, 1999).

Graff, Gary. "Britney Spears: The Queen of the Charts Talks Candidly." *Rolling Stone* online. (February 26, 1999).

Lanham, Tom. Review, *...Baby, One More Time. Entertainment Weekly* online. (January 12, 1999).

The *Rolling Stone* online service was used to obtain the following bios: Britney Spears, Madonna, Mariah Carey, Whitney Houston, Backstreet Boys, 'N Sync.

TV Guide. Transcript of Online Chat with Britney Spears. (March 29, 1999).

Photo Credits

All Action/Retna Limited U.S.A.: ©Dave Hogan: pp. 37 top, 51, 64-65, 72, 89, 91; ©Suzan Moore: p. 36 **David Allocca/DMI:** pp. 78, 79, 80-81 **Alpha/Globe Photos, Inc.:** ©Mark Allan: pp. 20, 21, 27, 29, 30, 33, 43, 67 **Art Resource:** p. 32 left **Corbis:** ©Pacha: p. 69 **Ron Galella Ltd.:** ©Peter Kramer: pp. 58-59, 62; ©Jim Smeal: p. 70 **Globe Photos Inc.:** ©Fitzroy Barrett: pp. 6, 38, 82, 88 **London Features International, Ltd. U.S.A.:** ©David Fisher: pp. 73, 84; ©Melvin Jones: p. 22; ©Jen Lowery: pp. 47, 54, 86; ©Dennis Van Tine: p. 76; ©UAZ: p. 83 **Photofest:** p. 17 **Retna Limited U.S.A.:** ©Steve Granitz: pp. 25, 37 bottom, 40, 50; ©Tim Hale: p. 23; ©Bernard Kuhmstedt: pp. 53, 55; ©Eddie Malluk: pp. 75, 94; ©Joseph Marzullo: p. 61; ©Walter McBride: p. 9; ©Ernie Paniccioli: pp. 2, 5, 12, 15, 18, 19, 32 right, 42, 44, 60, 66, 77, 93; ©Redferns/Call: p. 24;©Kelly A. Swift: pp. 57, 87 **Star File Photo:** ©Roger Glazer: p. 14; ©Alex Lloyd Gross: pp. 35, 45; ©Todd Kaplan: pp. 11, 48

WRITE TO BRITNEY

Britney Spears
c/o Britney Fan Club
PO Box 7022
Red Bank, NJ 07701-7022

The Britney Spears Fan Club
PO Box 250
Osyka, MS 39657

Britney Spears Websites
The Britney Spears official website:
www.peeps.com/britney
Email Britney at: britney@peeps.com